CRADLE of FORESTRY

ISBN-13: 978-0-15-366962-0
ISBN-10: 0-15-366962-4

3 4 5 6 7 8 9 10   805   13 12 11 10 09 08

Harcourt

SCHOOL PUBLISHERS

Visit *The Learning Site!* www.harcourtschool.com

THE CRADLE OF FORESTRY

The area around the Biltmore Forest School became North Carolina's first national forest, as well as the first national forest created by Congress. It was called the Pisgah National Forest. Mount Pisgah is in the center.

Many years later, in 1968, the area within the Pisgah National Forest where Schenck had his school was set aside as the Cradle of Forestry. By protecting these areas, Congress told everyone that forests need to be valued.

Today, the Cradle of Forestry has more than 6,000 acres of land. Thousands of visitors come here every year. They hike on the area's trails. They learn about the forest.

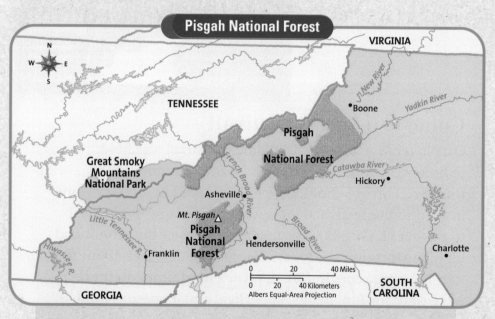

Pisgah National Forest

VIRGINIA

TENNESSEE

New River

Boone

Yadkin River

Pisgah

National Forest

Catawba River

Great Smoky
Mountains
National Park

French Broad River

Hickory

Asheville

Little Tennessee R.

Mt. Pisgah

Pisgah
National
Forest

Hendersonville

Broad River

Charlotte

Hiwassee R.

Franklin

0   20   40 Miles

0   20   40 Kilometers
Albers Equal-Area Projection

SOUTH
CAROLINA

GEORGIA

The Cradle of Forestry is within the Pisgah National Forest.

CRADLE of FORESTRY

Printed in Mexico

ISBN-13: 978-0-15-366962-0
ISBN-10: 0-15-366962-4

3 4 5 6 7 8 9 10   805   13 12 11 10 09 08

Harcourt
SCHOOL PUBLISHERS

Visit *The Learning Site!* www.harcourtschool.com

FORESTS OF NORTH CAROLINA

The history of western North Carolina is connected to its forests. Thousands of acres of forest surround vast mountain ranges in this part of the state. The Blue Ridge Mountains divide the Piedmont region from the Mountain region. They are part of the larger Appalachian Range. This range goes from Canada to the Great Smoky Mountains.

Large rivers flow through North Carolina's forests and mountains. The French Broad River flows from North Carolina to Tennessee. More than 200 miles long, it is a popular place for white-water rafting. Near the French Broad River is a tall peak called Mount Pisgah.

Mount Pisgah at daybreak

The forests of North Carolina are filled with trees.

Two kinds of trees grow here. One kind is broadleaf trees. A broadleaf tree has wide, flat leaves. These leaves change color and drop off each fall. Oak trees are examples of these kinds of trees. This area is home to many oaks. There are also hickory, maple, and yellow poplar trees.

Needleleaf trees, the other kind of tree, have thin, sharp leaves. They stay green all year. Pine trees are the most common example of these trees in the mountain forests.

Long ago, American Indians lived in these forests and mountains. They hunted and farmed here. Many animals, such as black bears, red foxes, deer, and rabbits, all live in this part of North Carolina.

Red foxes live in the forests.

CHANGES FOR THE MOUNTAIN REGION

Europeans came to this area in the late 1700s. At first, most of these newcomers lived in the valleys. Life in the mountains was too hard. The land there was not good for growing crops. Moving goods into the mountains from the cities was difficult.

In the late 1800s, North Carolina's population began to grow. Soon forest products were in high demand in cities and towns. Many forests in other parts of the country had already been cut down. Great forests of the Appalachian Mountains had been cut down and sold. In the Midwest, too, forests had been destroyed.

The rocky soil of the Mountain region made growing crops difficult.

Railroads made it easier to take lumber from the mountains to the cities.

Then an important change came to western North Carolina. A railroad was built through the North Carolina mountains. The railroad made it much easier for wood and other resources to be transported to big cities. Loggers came to cut down the trees. By the early 1900s, the forests of North Carolina were badly damaged.

Around the same time, a wealthy man named George Vanderbilt had an idea for a way to save the forests. He bought many large areas of land in the mountains. He planned to build a large home, called the Biltmore House, in this area. Because he owned the land, loggers could not come in and cut down the trees in his forests.

RESCUING A FOREST

Vanderbilt hired a man named Gifford Pinchot (PIN•choh) to manage his land. Pinchot had studied forestry in Europe. Forestry is the science of managing and protecting forests and forest resources.

Pinchot convinced Vanderbilt to buy more land in the area. Vanderbilt bought more than 100,000 acres of land, including Mount Pisgah. But soon, Pinchot left to work for the government. He became the first head of the United States Forest Service.

To take Pinchot's place, Vanderbilt hired Dr. Carl Schenck. Like Pinchot, Schenck had studied forestry in Europe.

George Vanderbilt

Gifford Pinchot

Biltmore Forest School Clubhouse

Schenck worked for Vanderbilt for 14 years. He worked to turn the woods around Mount Pisgah into a healthy forest again.

This was a difficult task. Many of the trees had been cut down. The forest ecosystem was badly damaged. Many of the animals and insects no longer lived there. To fix this, Schenck had to renew the soil. He had to replant many trees and other plants. This was the true beginning of forest conservation in America.

While he was making the Pisgah forests healthy again, Schenck started a school called the Biltmore Forest School. The school was in an old community schoolhouse. Classes began to meet in 1898.

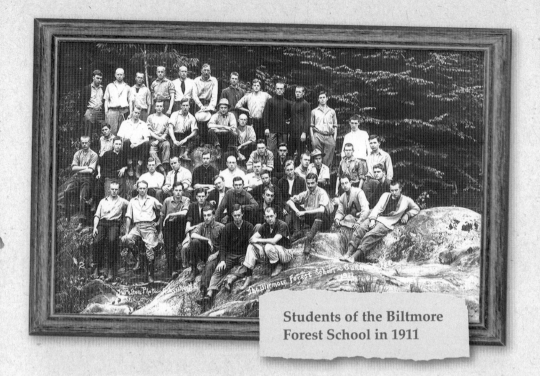

Students of the Biltmore
Forest School in 1911

LEARNING FROM THE FOREST

Students came to this special school to learn about forestry. They studied the many kinds of trees and other plants of the forest. They learned about lumbering. They learned how to keep the forest healthy and strong.

The Biltmore Forest School was the first forestry school in the United States. It was open for more than ten years. About 300 students attended classes there. Schenck's students did not just learn from books. They learned by working in the forest itself.

In 1909, Schenck left his job, but he did not close his school. Instead, he held forestry classes around the world. He taught in Germany, Switzerland, and France.

Finally, in 1913, Schenck decided it was time to close the Biltmore Forest School. But his work would not be forgotten. It was just the beginning of modern conservation. Conservation is the protection and wise use of natural resources, such as trees. Today, many of Schenck's ideas about conservation are still being used.

When Schenck closed the Biltmore Forest School, Gifford Pinchot was working for President Theodore Roosevelt. Pinchot wanted to honor Schenck for his work in protecting forests. At his request, government officials set aside a large area of forest where Schenck had worked.

Come to a Forest Festival!

On November 26–29, 1908, a forest festival was held to honor the tenth anniversary of the founding of the Biltmore Forest School. People interested in forestry were invited to the festival. Horse-drawn carriages took guests to the event. Guests were taken on tours of the school and on hikes through the forest. There were lectures about the latest experiments in forestry. For entertainment, there were outdoor luncheons, speeches, and a possum hunt.

THE CRADLE OF FORESTRY

The area around the Biltmore Forest School became North Carolina's first national forest, as well as the first national forest created by Congress. It was called the Pisgah National Forest. Mount Pisgah is in the center.

Many years later, in 1968, the area within the Pisgah National Forest where Schenck had his school was set aside as the Cradle of Forestry. By protecting these areas, Congress told everyone that forests need to be valued.

Today, the Cradle of Forestry has more than 6,000 acres of land. Thousands of visitors come here every year. They hike on the area's trails. They learn about the forest.

The Cradle of Forestry is within the Pisgah National Forest.

The Forest Discovery Center

Inside the Forest Discovery Center

When people visit the Cradle of Forestry today, there are many ways for them to learn about the history of this special place. At the Forest Discovery Center, visitors can watch a movie about the history of the Pisgah National Forest. They can learn about the people who played important roles in the area's growth.

The Forest Discovery Center has hands-on exhibits for visitors to enjoy. They can learn about managing forests. They can also learn about the goals of forest conservation. They can see how forest workers do their jobs today. They can play a computer game that challenges them to make their own decisions about land management.

EXPLORING THE FOREST

   Visitors of all ages can enjoy walking tours around the Cradle of Forestry. The Biltmore Campus Tour offers visitors a chance to learn about the forest and the school. It is also a trip back to the early 1900s. Visitors see the one-room schoolhouse where Biltmore students had their classes. They pass a general store, a blacksmith shop, a garden, and cabins where students lived.

   On the Forest Festival Tour people learn about early forestry experiments and today's forest issues. They also see an old sawmill.

Visitors hike on trails through the Cradle of Forestry.

Ladybugs are arthropods.

The Pink Beds

The Forest Discovery Trail is the longest walking tour. On this tour, a guide takes visitors along a grassy path deep inside the forest. They experience what the students at the Biltmore Forest School did every day.

Vistors can see many different plants and animals on these tours. Many types of arthropods live in the forest. Arthropods are animals whose bodies are divided into sections. They also have many jointed legs. Ladybugs and centipedes are two of the arthropods living in the forest.

Other plants and wildlife can be found in a nearby valley called the Pink Beds. In the spring and summer, it is filled with pink wildflowers.

FUN IN THE FOREST

The Cradle of Forestry is a great place to see migrating birds. Looking up, visitors might see ducks, geese, swans, songbirds, and hawks. The birds often stop in this area to rest on their spring and fall journeys.

Many people go camping in the Pisgah National Forest. Campers can stay in campgrounds throughout the forest. The many lakes and rivers are good for boating.

Young visitors to the Cradle of Forestry have plenty to do, too. There are scavenger hunts, "fact safaris," and puppet shows. There are also games about wilderness life. One game explores the food chain. Another follows a bird's migration, showing many dangers the bird faces along the way.

People wait to race their kayaks and canoes on the French Broad River.

A robin near her nest in the Pisgah National Forest.

Students at the Cradle of Forestry Center

Students can participate in educational programs. These programs teach students about monitoring the ozone and about organisms that live in water.

Visitors to the Cradle of Forestry can attend classes, too. Some classes teach visitors how to plant trees and how to build trails and manage their land.

A visit to the Cradle of Forestry is a chance to experience history. It is a chance to learn about nature and why protecting forests is important.

Think and Respond

1. What is the Cradle of Forestry?

2. Why did George Vanderbilt first buy land in the mountains of western North Carolina?

3. Why was the Biltmore Forest School important?

4. Why is conserving forests important?

5. How did the geography of the Mountain region influence the way people lived there?

Activity

With a partner, write a script for a tour of the Cradle of Forestry. Tell about the history of the place. Tell why it is such an important resource for the state. Then act out your tour for classmates.